The Al[chemy]
of Desire

Poems

Dianalee Velie

Plain View Press
http://plainviewpress.net

3800 N. Lamar, Suite 730-260
Austin, TX 78756

ISBN: 978-1-935514-05-3
Library of Congress Control Number: 2013935305

Cover Art: *Wood Thrushes in Love* by Roderick W. MacIver
http://www.herondance.org
Cover Design: Pam Knight

Other Books by Dianalee Velie

Soul Proprietorship: Women in Search of Their Souls, Plain View Press, 2010
The Many Roads to Paradise, Rock Village Publishing, 2006
First Edition, Rock Village Publishing, 2005
Glass House, Rock Village Publishing, 2004

Dianalee Velie
PO Box 290
Newbury, NH   03255
www.dianaleevelie.com

for

Bob

Come live with me and be my love,
And we will all the pleasures prove,
That valleys, groves, hills and fields,
Woods or steepy mountains yields.

"The Passionate Shepherd to His Love"

—Christopher Marlowe

Contents

I. *And not to have is the beginning of desire.*

II. *A desire fulfilled is sweet to the soul.*

III. *What makes the engine go? Desire, desire, desire.*

IV. *And so desire carries me along. "E cosi desio me mana."*

I.

And not to have
is the beginning of desire.

—Wallace Stevens

In the Beginning

—Inspired by Mark Twain's *The Diaries of Adam and Eve*

Talk about a new beginning!
One minute ago, I sat here a lump of dirt,
now I'm a man using these things I've labeled words,
words for my arms, my legs, my sky, my sun.
Me, It's all about me. Maybe I'll be the world's
first poet. Me! I write, I walk, I jump, I'm hungry,
I'm lonely, I'm silent, I'm wishing. Hmm…

Must be careful with that concept wishing.
The beautiful silence has disappeared.
I woke up with an ache in my side and there she sat,
sort of like me, yet really different. She can't stop talking
about something called emotions and a new word, we.
We should do this and we should do that.
What have I done? Now it's all about us.

Now she's gone and done it. Wished for other creatures.
They're all over the place. She especially loves
those things she calls cats. Arrogant little fur balls,
I hate them! The one that goes woof, though,
I've sort of adopted. He obeys me like I thought she would.
I've named this one dog, the opposite of that guy up there
christening himself God and calling all the shots down here.

Also, a few of these other animals are making me salivate,
I wonder... I could use a little more than nuts and berries
and those plants she's started to chop up into something
she calls a salad. But, to tell you the truth, it's that slinky
creature curled around the apple tree that's hypnotizing her.
Trust me that one's going to cause trouble in Paradise.
Genius that I am, I think I'll start my novel with that scene.

It will be my masterpiece. It will be my Genesis.
Everyone will know my name.

Fragments

They stick out, secure in their pain,
draining their red wine like a splinter
draws blood. Wearing a haunted look,
they watch embracing couples dance
until, threatening tears, their eyes turn
to stare blankly at the floral centerpiece.

Widowed, divorced, separated and alone,
they pick up their forks, toy with their food
and make another trip to the ladies room
to brush their hair, take deep breaths
and check the time. They are fragments
in a wanting world of complete couples,

nibbling sweet slivers of wedding cake,
a prominent sign this endured evening
is, thankfully, about to come to an end.

Domestication

My daughter-in-law thinks I've raised a gem:
her dear husband who loves to cook and clean,
my domestic skills an endearing emblem
of how I raised him. I smile, serene.

His laundry tasks are quite meticulous
and whites stay away from multi-color.
The bread is always perfect, ravenous
folks agree, whole grained and full of flavor.

My son, Mr. Wonderful, because of me?
Honestly, these traits I do not possess.
But I suspect the reason is simply
when he was eight, I now will confess,

I turned his white hockey stockings hot pink
and burned the bread as black as India-ink.

Parallel Flight Plans

In a hotel suite in Los Angeles
we catch up on our separate busy
lives. Two adult sisters, one childless,
the other a new grandmother, agree

our morning walk to Starbucks sanctifies
this time together. A yearly business
trip coincides with a grandson's first cries.
Today, career woman and poetess

board two different planes to their desires:
one to New York and her fashion career,
one to Boston, then on to New Hampshire's
mountains and lakes and written words of sheer

joy. Flying home on parallel flight plans,
their sibling bond fills the huge blue expanse.

Dianalee Velie

Chicken Farmer I Still Love You

—Newbury, New Hampshire

I want to live here forever, stop time
near the graffitied rock still declaring,
"Chicken Farmer I Still Love You." Sublime,
in this town where efforts at removing

this undying sentiment meet with wild
unexpected protests, though no one knows
when this vow first appeared. My bold child,
you stand, icon of love, with golden rows

of flowers beneath hard stone words. Lovers
stop, smile or weep, every passing day,
wishing for passion on four leaf clovers,
each one hopeful, in their own private way,

like me, the poet, singing out your name,
clutching a photo, my heart still aflame.

Carrot Muffin

Any given form comes and goes in a process of time,
for any given time is temporary.
                    —Ernest Holmes

Loaded with calories, carbs and other
countless sweets, as well as the carrots,
I hope will fulfill my daily vegetable
requirement, I inhale this chock full
of everything muffin, on the run,
as usual, filling this abyss in my belly,
dreaming of sitting down with some
delectable bounty on the silver plate
it deserves, pink peonies in a crystal
vase upon the table, tea poured from
a porcelain pot, a white linen napkin,
starched and neatly unfolded, laid
upon my lap, sitting across from...

Here my fantasy stops, dead,
my memory searching desperately
to bring back a living picture
of you: black curly hair, tight jeans
and cowboy boots, a mischievous
look in your coffee colored eyes,
laughter always tickling
your lips, your lips always tickling
that favorite spot on my neck,
this world, too briefly, our playground.

But, here I sit, brushing leftover crumbs
into a brown paper bag to feed
to the wild sparrows, the sustaining
of any life, so precious, so precarious,
since your loss diminished my world.
Grateful and graceful, eager
for the generous hand out,
the birds congregate at my feet,
momentarily filling the void,
until, tidbits gone, they disappear,
like your image, so very real
a few moments ago, smiling at me
from some unfathomable place in time.

Conference Call

The white bone of my forehead presses against
the cold white shower tiles, my thin pale skin

the only thing separating me from mourning.
I allow this liquid lover to caress my body,

swirling remnants of grief down the drain.
Grabbing for a bleached towel to wrap around

my dripping body, I run for the ringing phone,
trying to ignore the alienated, red, heart-shaped

hot-tub in this hotel room of mauves and greens,
an unexpected garish display shrieking of loneliness.

Then laughter fills the room, bouncing from cell
tower to cell tower, as I describe to a friend

my surroundings at this conference center,
the penalty, of this tub, the price I must pay

for late registration. Sitting on the edge
of this premeditated for passion relic,

my laughter silenced with a click,
I listen to words still hanging in the air

from years ago, words suddenly drifting
into the room by celestial conference call:

The cats and dogs are fine, Darling.
I miss you. Hurry home. I'm waiting.

Mirage in May

And let me ask you this. The dead, where aren't they?
—Franz Wright

With winter blue pants, rolled up, and now wet,
he wades with her into the sea. His shirt
hugs a bouncing belly. Their old eyes flirt
with delight. This joy, I fear, I forget.

Mottled hands hold tightly. Her free right hand
lifts high, a dripping, grandmotherly dress
above plump, bowed knees. Welcome waves caress
and splash bare shins, swirling the soft warm sand,

this enchantment misting me with sea spray,
and childlike joy so contagious, for
a moment time teeters. In the gap, your
hand takes mine. This sudden mirage in May,

so real, I feel your touch and believe we
have grown old together. As sure as this
couple play right here, a pure magic kiss
drifts through infinity with symmetry

and you kiss me, then fade away. I'm left
with no footprints on the beach, only dreams
of past ebbing tides lured out by moonbeams,
receding, remote, cold-blue and bereft.

He Says

He says he lost his twenties: chewed up
by medical school and internship.
He says he belongs to the clean plate club,
enjoying everything put on his dish.

He says he'd like to see me again.

I am absorbing our conversation,
like polish on tarnished silver,
as the talk shifts to quantum physics
and the power of the observer.

I observe my heart tinkering with trust,
something I had misplaced long ago.
On guard, I ask if he is married.
His answer: Yes, is that a problem?

It is, and it is not, simultaneously.
We have encountered only this event,
solid and substantial with unexplored
variants waiting behind closed doors.

So I slide him to a safe distance, like
the piece of Chocolate Decadence Cake,
after I have devoured three tempting mouthfuls,
regretfully pushing my plate across the table,

still craving so much more.

Cold Desire

On Ile San Louis, overlooking
Notre Dame, in December, I observe
the ice cream lovers sitting on the bank
of the Seine, the flying buttresses
crowning their cold desire.
They sprinkle sweetened kisses
upon each others' muffled ears,
bundled, scarfed necks and
frosty pink cheeks, while nibbling
each others' ice cream cones,
lips scarlet with icy cravings.

She swings her legs, encased
in long, brown suede boots,
up across his lap and he grabs
her waist in another embrace,
and a kiss, lasting so long,
I have to look away.
When I gaze up and out
the steamy window
of the Café Fleur en Ile,
the cold couple climbs
on their scooter, ready

to head into the bright lights
of Paris, lights twinkling
in my tears, where the cold
of their lips, the cold
of their fingertips,
melts the cold
of my frozen heart.

Fog

The fog fell in shrouds obscuring vision,
so not until the last moment did we
see the void, the empty, gaping incision
where happiness used to dwell: family.

Gone: the tiles stained with your youthful blood
and the orange tree whose fruit we juiced.
Gone: the sand box, now, a pile of mud
on a bare lot where mist and tears are fused.

You walk the wet property, picking up
a ceramic shard, a stray violet:
fragments of a life. Songs of a cherub
float in the haze, a soft wafting couplet:

My love, feel our moist kisses sweep your brow,
to guide you forever, our divine vow.

Dianalee Velie

Spinach

Strength is born in the deep silence of long-suffering hearts;
not amidst joy.

—Felicia Hemans, English poet

I craved spinach this morning, desired
    it for breakfast more than sex. Boiling
emerald bouquets by bunches, I viewed, in the viridian
    water, the stagnant pond of my past.

Jaded with grief,
    I gobbled the slimy green leaves,
as if it they were my last meal,
    knowing they were yours.

I even drank down the gritty potion
    left behind,
this cathartic cleansing still
    creating no closure.

The autopsy report left no disclaimer:
    Stomach contents: spinach, undigested,
unfinished, like your life, ended on an endless day
    two days before our anniversary,

a day when two dozen white roses,
    assumed funeral condolences,
arrived with the mourners
    and your hand written card.

Fragile as the ice encrusted tree limbs
    snapping in this frozen February,
my heart hardened and cracked, unforgiving
    of your anniversary greeting from the grave,

unforgiving of this veritable vegetable,
        the only truth you took with you,
unforgiving of these iron rich edible leaves
        strengthening me with ritualistic pleasure

and its companion   pain.   I devoured
        these tear soaked stems and leaves,
nourished by the thought that our very potency
        is stolen from the envious earth of your decay.

Unchained

On the dock at Mallory Square,
a contortionist, with snake-
like movements, slips out of yards
of heavy chains, handcuffs and locks,
all wrapped around his body by tourists
enjoying the show while waiting
for the sun to set on Key West.

Spreading a golden carpet across
the warm waters of the Atlantic Ocean,
the sun god sinks into the sea, a seductive
tease, tempting us to walk on water
with him, to leave this dark side of paradise,
made even darker by the power
outage that has blackened the Key.

The charcoal sky settles swiftly,
surrounding us with black. The clouds,
having caused this surreal sunset,
now hold the moon and stars hostage.
Filling my lungs with moist dark
air, I inhale the night sky as it turns
as smooth as black patent leather.

Even though all the restaurants
have closed, the bartender
at The Hog's Breath Saloon
stays open, accepting only cash,
tending bar by candle light and refilling
bowls of pretzels as everyone drinks
in this instant intimacy of darkness.

Above me, in a banyan tree,
a confused rooster crows,
begging for the light, his confusion
blending with the soothing sounds
of *Ave Maria* played by a lone
entertainer on his simple wooden flute:
a contra puntal, clash of sounds.

Like the unchained performer,
my soul twists like a snake
around memories of Eden,
a time before the disappearance
of happiness. For the moment,
I am unfettered, free of grief,
crowing, like the rooster,

for a new dawn, faithful
I will find my way in the dark.

In My Garden

The blue jay mocks my naive attempts at pulling up wildroot.
Neat little bouquets of green and white leaves that,
I want there,
Not here
Placed like words on a page
Ordered and pleasant to my eye.
But the jay has consulted with the wren to mock me
And I am through for today
Trying to tame wildroot.

Portrait of the Poet

For my portrait, I must be nude,
bared for the artist to see the scars
of body and psyche that have curtailed
my desire. An open book of poetry
will lie beside me with a sleeping cat
upon the printed page. Nearby, a blue
pen rests upon a folded sheet of ivory
paper, concealing an abandoned poem.
A bouquet of fragrant gardenias will
fill the room with scent while
three white memorial candles illuminate
my space, casting the ever-present,
incandescent shadows of my life.

I must face away from the artist,
my long mahogany hair the focus,
spilling away from the curve of my back,
not my emerald eyes, deep with sorrow.
My left hand, ringless, supports me,
as I lean into the sway of my hair,
making visible the closure of a necklace
at the nape of my neck, suggesting pearls
hanging languidly between my breasts,
teasing the voyeur, who will stare
at this painting in the future, when I am
old, or dead, yearning to unlock
this poem's intricate clasp.

Dianalee Velie

Abenaki Morning Prayer

Lake Sunapee, New Hampshire

Each day I greet the people of the dawn.
Abenaki maidens lift the black sky,
kwai-kwai, they whisper gently, as I yawn,

asking what new wonders this day will spawn.
I compose, in reverence, my reply:
each day I greet the people of the dawn,

with thanks for the sunrise lighting my lawn,
for this translucent glow, *woli-woni*.
Kwai-kwai, they whisper gently, as I yawn,

look now to the ridge to face the young fawn,
one quick glance and you'll see his white tail fly.
Each day I greet the people of the dawn,

as they share their visions, I, a mere pawn
of this elegant life, this gift to untie.
Kwai-kwai, they whisper gently, as I yawn.

Noiselessly, like the night, they have withdrawn.
This day provides a real present, I sigh.
Each day I greet the people of the dawn.
Kwai-kwai, they whisper gently, as I yawn.

II.

A desire fulfilled is sweet to the soul.

—Proverbs 13:19

Morning Sacrament

—Block Island Communion

Oh Holy Caffeine, blessed first cup of coffee,
stirring my brain, swirling white, creamy consciousness
into the dark, deep unconscious with just one sip.

Morning drips into my veins as the sun rises
from beneath the sea, setting the kitchen on fire,
blessing me with this ordination of caffination.

Head bowed, my lips seek the well-worn rim
of my earthenware mug, the spot worn smooth
by mornings' continuous sacrament, as I contemplate
                              the contents of my fragile cup.

Why Poetry?

We write to taste life twice, in the moment
and in retrospection.
　　　　　　　　—Anais Nin

Awash in my wonderful world of words
wondering, *why poetry?* answers bloom
like purple tulips waiting to be plucked
and put into bouquets of stanzas
before flowering into seeming sense.

Poetry: to remember the salty sea-breeze
smell of my father's sandy hair and to forget
the feel of his gun metal coffin and
the haunting sound of taps played
by Marines at his military funeral,
followed by a blast of bullets in the air.

Poetry: to fill the gap left in my consciousness
with unconscious constant recognition
of the vulnerability of life when husband
followed father into the unknown, the night
before feeding me a bite of his lobster,
dripping butter down my lips that he kissed.

Poetry: to describe in detail my grandson's
upturned, arrogant two-year-old smile and
that darling dimple in his right cheek
that everyone will envision, verifying the
reason for making form out of his
formlessness, new life out of his death.

Poetry: to chisel carefully crafted phrases
into the granite of memory,
epitaphs on the vault of the printed page,
allowing me to live life twice, the second time
preserved, no longer private, punctuated
with finality, the finality to defy even death
by keeping alive momentous moments.

Poetry: to fulfill the need to dominate
and control the uncontrollable,
placing words on page after page,
seeking some illumination,
as I succumb, survive and savor,
succumb, survive and savor,
again and again, every blessing
in this mystery called life.

The Birth of Double Digits

She, a silky six,
He, a ramrod seven,
Tonight
Unite at eight:
By nine conceive ten.

Wolf

This time his cross-dressing was out of hand.
As soon as she crawled into the four poster bed,
the bed that had been in her family for generations,
she noticed the frilly nightcap. Pulling the covers back,
she stared at the wolf in granny's nightdress.

She thought this relationship was different.
He had guided her through the dark forest
of her divorce, even at one point carrying
her load. Never, should she have let him
into her home and then her broken heart.

It began with her red cape. Like an animal,
he said it excited him, and asked her to twirl
and whirl for him until he collapsed in a frenzy.
Soon he was doing the spinning, using the cape
like a matador, coming in for the kill.

Funny, at first, though a little odd, she should
have cut if off when he wanted to wear
her undies, but part of her loved a bad boy,
enjoyed their kinky play, but granny's night dress,
this took her way out of her comfort zone.

That hungry look in his eyes, though, always
swayed her. He said he wanted to devour her
and smothered her in kisses, I can eat you
he howled and she totally surrendered.
Her screams excited him and his yowling grew.

Coming to pick up the kids for the weekend,
her ex-husband, the hunter, found them
entangled in granny's bed, and well,
you saw the headlines that became a fairy tale,
you know the rest of the story.

Campus Highlights

Highlighted by the sun for a moment,
a campus building suddenly outshines
the ruby maple, a fall requirement,
highlighted by the sun for a moment,
so briefly, seconds ago, enjoyment
spilling from her branches like rich red wines.
Highlighted by the sun for a moment,
a campus building suddenly outshines

all else, illuminated by the student
in her dorm, head on her boyfriend's lap,
reading *Paradise Lost*, very content.
All else, illuminated by the student,
enraptured by God and this assignment:
the calm of love after sex and a nap.
All else, illuminated by the student
in her dorm, head on her boyfriend's lap.

Dianalee Velie

Elegy for Juan

Carefully crafted words dance
a tango with Latin intensity,
an intensity unrestrained
by two foreign languages.

Our naked skins converse
like memorized song,
comprehension as
clear as the Caribbean.

More powerful than speech,
the scents of hibiscus and jasmine
linger with the salty, lime taste
of tequila on our breaths.

Above the seductive sound
of the sea, the Goddess Ix-chel
christens this scene with her full moon,
when the vision serpent enters.

With his obsidian lancet,
he stabs the moment with thought.
Not willing to sacrifice, I fight desire:
Do not let this become a poem.

But, the sliver of an elegy
is embedded in my heart and
the words always win, powerful,
eager oracles ready to portend.

Spirit of Lake George

Summer in the world—
floating on waves
in the lake.
                    —Basho

Silent heart-shaped shimmering chimes frolic
above sacramental waters for hours
a lattice of birch leaves so symbolic

of our need to laugh through catastrophic
private and public events, now ours.
Silent heart-shaped shimmering chimes frolic

for sacramental waters where orphic
pleasures dilute sorrow in these bowers,
a lattice of birch leaves so symbolic,

of our quest for pleasure. Here bucolic
stands of birches cling to rock that empowers.
Silent heart-shaped shimmering chimes frolic,

catch the light and joy so tragicomic,
we are heedless of upcoming showers.
A lattice of birch leaves, so symbolic,

captures our Spirit, now so idyllic
we are certain of angelic powers.
Silent heart-shaped shimmering chimes frolic:
a lattice of birch leaves so symbolic.

A Mystical Movement

The comforting fog spreads a gossamer veil
over the blushing colors of fall oaks,
trees preparing to cast off their royal
foliage like bashful brides dropping red
nightgowns before welcoming snow-white sheets.

Yesterday's borrowed blue sky stays hidden,
tucked safely away like a handkerchief,
welcoming this misty day of autumn's
tears, this cushion of clouds obscuring sun.
A calm day to celebrate creation,

the earth's goodness and nature's mysteries.
In this holiness of being so wedded
to my thoughts, I hear the processional
bridal chorus from Wagner's Lohengrin.
This whistled, windy movement skims the lake

like a memory, until you appear,
my true knight, drawn by a swan, just a glimpse,
and you are shrouded again, returning
into the past, knowing I will follow,
soon, but not yet my love, not yet, not yet...

"A Process in the Weather of the Heart"

—Dylan Thomas

Wild and wicked, winter winked at spring
    before flaunting his final serious fling.

Spring watched with exhilaration and awe
    as a cold world trembled and trees bowed before

his total domination of pure white,
    his bluster so charming on this March night.

Secure, she smiled, demure, not forlorn,
    he would simply melt when croci were born.

Quickly followed by hyacinths, tulips
    and more, then dogwoods and blossoms their lips

would explore. Their time together never
    lengthy, when seasons intertwine, clever,

but often messy. She soon would forget
    his cold zeal and, forever fickle, let

summer melt her cool reserve, while fall
    rustled, chilling the new north wind, his call

destined to quell the hot, rapturous earth.
    Patiently winter plans his cold rebirth,

plotting his wild and wicked returns,
    stripping fall bare, while in his heart he yearns

        for spring.

Bad Date.Com

The blue clown wig really didn't cut it,
nor did the big red balloon to really
mark his presence, but worse, the nit-wit
who kept his hat on to hide, least I see,

his total baldness. Better yet, a twelve-step
AA lecture while I choked on a glass
of wine inhibited any windswept
romance from occurring with this upper class

loner. Their edges blur, but extreme guilt
over a wife's suicide is not first date
conversation. Under that bed quilt
I dare not venture. I'd rather hibernate.

But one kudo to the man, who likes them fat
saying I'd look better in a 250-pound format.

Pomegranate Tree in Paradise

Clipped wings, or not,
her beloved bird attempted
to fly, to nestle on her shoulder,
his sweetest place in the world,
sweeter than the faint memory
of a pomegranate tree in the tropics.

But, he landed on the floor,
helpless to return to his cage
or reach his adored destination.
His archrival, her new husband,
placed the bird's jungle gym
on the floor, where he gladly
climbed aboard before charging
the hand that helped him.

This bird knows envy.
To this man she has given wings
to glide above grief, this man
who snuggles now beside her,
kissing her crimson lips,
restorative and fruitful
as a pomegranate tree in paradise.

Mrs. Wakefield

—After the short story, *Wakefield*, by E.L. Doctorow

Did he think I couldn't see him, hiding above the garage?
At first, I laughed, wondering how long my husband's silliness
would last, then weariness of his stupidity, changed to anger.

The longer this continued, the more accustomed I became
to being alone. I dressed and undressed, purposely, in front
of the bedroom's big bay window, knowing he was watching.

My career flourished as I tossed my wife hat wantonly
to the wind. I watched him get shaggier daily, grow
long shabby hair and go unshaven, thinking he was hidden.

In the beginning, I tossed enough food scraps in the garbage
to sustain life, his, but then I left with the children
for two weeks. Let him live like a tramp and try to survive.

When we returned, I felt violated to see traces of his hair
in the shower. Soon, his dear friend, Dirk, began coming
to dinner, often to console me, more often to seduce.

Then last night, he stayed and I drew the curtains shut.
My greatest delight: the footprints in the snow outside the bedroom
window and the click, click, click of the unlit propane pilot.

The police were sympathetic. "So much sorrow, Ma'am.
First the disappearance of your husband, and now,
your garage burned to the ground by arson.

These footprints match those of a vagrant seen lurking
around the clinic next door. We've had our eyes on him."
I offered the officer a sweet, timid smile of thanks.

Since it was Saturday, we all went to a movie.
No need to hang around, I had parked
the S.U.V. nowhere near the garage.

Falling into a reassuring sleep that night
in Dirk's arms, I jumped out of bed, swearing
I heard Wakefield's voice, hurling out these hot words,
"Honey, I'm home."

Holy Discord

Hatred stirreth up strifes: but love covereth all sins.
—Proverbs 10:12

The Avenging Angel screamed, destroy everything in sight!

> She did not feed the hungry.
> She did not clothe the poor.
> She rarely kept the Sabbath.
> Destroy all this, for sure.

And her Defending Angel cried, but yet, she did love.

> In her heart she murdered twice.
> In her thoughts the serpent of fear.
> Her boundaries always bent for others.
> Destroy all this! Do you not hear?

And her Defending Angel sighed, but yet, she did love.

> Well, where is the earth's bounty?
> Where is everything she shared?
> How could she live so blindly?
> Did she only pretend to care?

And her Defending Angel wept, but yet, she did love.

> I will destroy where her eyes did not glance.
> Destroy what her mind did not seek.
> Destroy what she's never touched,
> For all the promises she could not keep.

And her Defending Angel smiled, but yet, she did love.

Did you see those hugs of empathy?
See them multiply ten fold.
See them spread throughout humanity.
Their end cannot be foretold.

And the Avenging Angel sighed, ah, yes, she did love.

Even as you listen,
she's stilled your vengeful sword.
I see your shoulders relax,
through out this holy discord.

And the Avenging Angel smiled, ah, yes, she did love.

I will stop this foolish discourse.
I'll spare this planet of pain.
Let her go on loving others.
See if she finds anything there to gain.

And the Defending Angel smiled, ah, yes, that she will love.

Exalting the X Chromosome

—For Vivienne

Clouds of creamy hydrangeas
and exuberant daisies
smiled to us from every room,
a calming womanly welcome
to this country farm house
where you placed the Adirondack
chairs in a semi-circle around
the outdoor fireplace,
a soft receptive curve, from you,
a woman we have never met.

On the worn wooden table inside,
we found bagels and bialys,
white fish from a Manhattan deli,
and homemade lox: gifts
so feminine of heart
they sheltered us under a canopy
of maternal love. Beneath this
protective aura, three sister travelers
lit the wood stove with the dry
split logs you had brought inside,

poured our libations and raised
our chalices to your presence,
exalting the X chromosome
with friendship and fine red wine.

Song of Spring

Sweet essential rain, liquid language
like falling glass, quenches the earth's thirst.

These delicate diamond drops,
resting on rosy-tipped birches,

set the White Mountains aflame.
Glittering in a scarlet sunset,

illuminating the hills in a ruby blaze,
the red mist worships the lingering sun.

Soon the moon will rise, raw and gorgeous,
over two thousand black shadows,

bouquets of darkness in early spring.
Sleeping beneath the birches,

softly awakened by the moist earth,
Persephone rises from her marriage bed,

the desire for illumination and a mother's
love so strong it escapes the confines

of womb or tomb. Showering her
on the eternally promised path

of birth and rebirth, raindrops rejoice
singing a song of spring.

Epiphany

The shrouding, weeklong fog had dissipated,
leaving my future reeling before me.
Like Sequanna, the Roman river goddess,
having fathomed abysmal turbulence
before winding her way back to tranquil seas,
this January Epiphany calmed and purified me.

For the first time in many nights, the North Star
pirouetted in the heavens, dancing an eternal ballet
for the moon, three kings, and me. In this season
of lengthening light and revelation, I emerged
from the lifting clouds, reassured, revitalized
and removed from fear. The welcomed, clear
arctic-wind chiseled the block of ice surrounding
my heart, sculpting a woman already in existence.

Winter's darkness had whittled away extraneous
crystals, revealing light within a familiar,
feminine figure. Arising with no gouges
from past pain, no hairline cracks
threatening to split, I resurfaced
from the river of rhetoric solid
as alabaster, yet as fluid as liquid silk,
quite mystified by my own transformation.

No longer placed on a pedagogic pedestal,
I materialized, poised in an unknown port of entry,
a humble, living statuette with written works
piled high on the palms of her outstretched hands,
spilling welcoming words into the cathartic
currents of the tributary called creation.

III.

What makes the engine go?

Desire, desire, desire.

—Stanley Kunitz

Jesus Greets Janis

He waits patiently at the Gates of Heaven
pleased with his sunset-hued, tie-dyed robes.
She stumbles in rubbing bloodshot eyes behind
her rose colored glasses, sure this is another
bad trip or a batch of bad bourbon.

Jesus smiles, grabs his guitar and plays
a couple of familiar riffs crooning, *take it,*
take another little piece of my heart now baby...
then signals for the angelic chorus to join in,
The seraphim really get down for a wild welcome.

Janis, not one to be denoted, wails back,
Oh Lord, won't you buy me a Mercedes Benz...
After a flying ovation, she realizes
she is not with the Kozmic Blues Band or
Big Brother and the Holding Company.

Work me, Lord, she whispers to Jesus,
looking for a stage and her psychedelic Porsche.
Jesus hands her a shot of Southern Comfort,
a drug free zone pin and a golden harp.
She plucks a few strings and sings to the Messiah

I Need a Man to Love. It's only about love here,
Jesus assures her as wardrobe fits her for a halo
and wings. Jesus whips out His Hohner harmonica.
Together, under the big sky dome, they belt out,
You know you got it, if makes you feel good...

Dianalee Velie

Searching the Shore for Jerusalem

Oh Beloved, take this raft quickly and lead it to shore.
                                        —Mirabai

I drift
        in the Dead Sea,
                searching the shore for Jerusalem.
I seduce
        sea, sky and sand,
                taming this trinity of temptations.
I float
        in amniotic waters
                gazing at reflections of life.
I bathe
        in unknown oceans,
                no horizon in view.
I gestate,
        a wandering womb
                mesmerized, summoning,

my body and soul chanting:
                deeper
                deeper
                deeper
I satiate
        this parched soul,
                searching for perfection.
I fade
        from sight, pure reflection,
                only now, a possibility.

I dive
> into my reservoir, as undisturbed
>> as a prophet's mirror.

I plunge
> into the precipice,
>> cast lines away until

I glimpse
> the glimmer, the glint,
>> the desire of a poem.

The Ecstasy of St. Theresa

—After the sculpture by Gian Lorenzo Bernini

Desiring my God, I surrendered
to the angel who entered my cloistered
cell, on his behalf, overwhelming me
with ecstasy. My passion, once set free,
exploded, could no longer be slaughtered.

With his golden spear the angel entered
my body and my soul. Lust, untempered,
filled me with fire: no apology.
Desiring my God, I surrendered.

I moaned in joy and pain, sweet words murmured
in thanksgiving for this blaze encountered
in my youth. Now approaching seventy,
I record in my diary sultry
memories of that day I faltered.
Desiring my God, I surrendered.

Desiring Heaven

A lake carries you into recesses of feeling otherwise impenetrable
—William Wordsworth

Desiring heaven,
warm water molecules,
held in the bosom of the lake
since summer, vaporize
into mist. Lured by the ice-
blue sky, they drift upward
inseparable from their source.

No fear of feeling foolish,
the rising mists play and dance
above the lake like angels
singing out the truth
of their intelligent design
with no contemplation
of their continual transformation.

Surrendering to nature,
resolved and faithful,
other water molecules
seek freedom to rest
in the frozen froth
building slowly
on the sandy shore.

No anger or irritation
at those who have risen,
only comfort at staying
put right now, to rise months,
or years later, peaceful
in the powerfulness
of their own being.

Flirting with winter,
insulated and warm
on the dock, only we wonder
if, when melt as we must
like the final flakes of snow,
we will witness the first
few shimmering snowdrops
of an additional spring.

Cold Gold

Gray mists whip across the lake from the west,
a cold-gold wind shaking down saffron leaves,
skittering across my deck with no rest.

Yesterday's warm sun dispensed small reprieves
from winter's looming, long, dark nights and cold
white days. A string of sparkling light achieves

my need to brighten up my world: Behold,
shadows smiling with unexpected joy.
Preparing for dormancy with untold

poems, my pen poised like a choirboy
ready to sing inside my cathedral,
I light a scented candle to enjoy

these last few days of wild autumnal
splendor, preparing to go within soon,
a content, prepared, dormant minstrel,

enchanted beneath a bold Hunter Moon.

And So Winter Begins

And so winter begins,
        questionable as
November skies
        until words tumble
from the air,
        like snowflakes,
piling into drifts
        of lines, then stanzas,
        poems blanketing
my world with meaning,
        a dreamscape portraying
deceptional pockets
        of silence.

Celestial connections
        of incandescence
permeate the night sky
        with promise.
Rooted to the earth with wonder,
        I gaze with curiosity
and longing, with such intensity,
        I become a star,
ready to yield
        each morning
to the crisp blank
        potential of dawn.

Blue Mountain Ecstasy

Against the backdrop of an ice blue sky,
bared and beautiful, the white birch welcomes
a plethora of blue jays squawking
thank yous for the scattered sunflower seeds
dotting the pristine blanket of new snow.

Deceptively declaring warmth, the sun
merely serves as a spotlight, christening
this icy scene of live cobalt glory,
this radiant reign of contagious joy,
this pure, perfect cinematic snapshot.

No camera in hand, I ponder words
pleading to preserve this apparition,
this burning birch ablaze in boastful blue,
this bright, blue, cold mountain of ecstasy,
this casual communion of nature,

so simple, so brief, so humble, so blue.

Dianalee Velie

The Scent of Wild Magnolias

We watched the inevitable destruction
from the eye of the hurricane.

This wretched weather.
These cursed workmen.
This hideous rain.

Gathering passion, the storm
heightened around us.

I need my deodorant.
Where's my brush?
Pour me more wine.

Wild winds whipped.
Visions blurred.

My family can't do that
to me anymore. I don't know
what I would do without him.

Her black eyes shine.
He flips seductive long hair.

The tempest intensifies, swirls like
an obsession, scenting the air with wild
magnolias unable to cling to their roots.

We watch lips shiver with new promise.
We watch lightning shatter the old.

Gala Affair

Did she know this would be her last gala affair
In this magnificent house, ablaze with laughter?
Vast quantities of alcohol uninhibit her guests
Over abundant trays of hors d'oeuvres. She disappears.
Resting her head on his shoulder, outdoors, she
Carefully memorizes the sight of the indoor lights.
Evening's star-scattered sky mimics the illuminated party.

Did she ever think this marriage would last?
Ever weary of the façade, she leans into his arms,
Cautiously at first, until they blend into the shadows,
Intimately promising each other better tomorrows.
Satisfied their spouses will be better off without them,
Infidelity beckons. A new paradise awaits exploration.
Old Promises break and scatter. Listening to the joyous
Noise, they rise, eager now to enter the valley of tears.

Dianalee Velie

Of Sparrows and Men

Baby sparrows have found a furrow
in the split rail fence,
a good first step.
The world is an uncertain place.
There are tanks rolling in the desert.
But not here, in the quiet of my backyard.
Here they see only the fence and the nest
they have just fled and the blood-red, sugar-water
mix meant for the hummingbirds
that enticed the babies to flee the nest,
enticed young men to volunteer and leave home.
I watch the sparrows and the boys on TV
and leave them both to cut scarlet roses,
no longer able to watch the deception
of sparrows and men.

Dandelions

Millions of slender purple stalks stand empty,
Shakespeare's little chimney sweeps

turned to silken, powder puffs of pollen dancing
in the air, feathery filigrees pollinating the earth,

placing dandelion seeds in places they never thought
they would be, like me, here in your home, washing

strawberries in your white porcelain sink,
imagining their discarded, rigid green stems

are diminutive soldiers standing at attention, surrounded
by miniature moats of blood-red, wasted berry tops,

an honor guard sounding silent taps beneath your faucet
on this Memorial Day, when heroes, lost in the winds of war,

are memorialized in cemeteries, flags planted and waving
alongside uniformed headstones, row after row after row,

where the dandelions are no longer brazen
yellow sweeps, but fluff floating everywhere,

even in the breeze outside your kitchen window,
disappearing like the days drifting behind us,

carrying two wounded hearts someplace,
somewhere, they thought they would never go.

Body Parts

Images of her ovaries float
before me on the doctor's screen,
the resting place of half the genetic
makeup of possible grandchildren
hidden in marshmallowy looking
orbs of potential parent.

Declared healthy, and accessible,
no shadows block the other genetic
half, linked to my son,
from completing their voyage,
their charge of desire,
and then division with purpose.

Purpose, what new purpose
do I possess as my own same
body parts wind slowly down?
Shrinking within me into little seeds
of longing, they stretch out their roots,
seeking streams of consciousness.

Never fearing drought,
fruitful, their stored energy
saturates me with insight
and a welcoming hint
of wisdom: the conception
of dreams delivered.

Bar Harbor Fortune

I don't need your answered prayers or the chains your lover wears.
I don't need your rings of gold or the secrets that you hold.
—Bruce Springstein

Grabbing my hand,
you pull me across the street
to the Psychic's front door.
She allows us three questions
for ten dollars apiece. Sequestered,
behind her closed curtains,
we both ask, independently,
about love, career and finances.

Later, comparing our futures
over cold shrimp and red wine,
you play a Tony Bennett CD
and we watch the setting sun
spread a golden pathway
to the Porcupine Islands,
highlighting only swaying lobster boats
and the sound of lapping waves.

This is where, one would think,
the romance begins, but
sliding into our respective beds,
we open our books and read,
like an old married couple, content
just knowing the other is there,
occasionally chatting about
thoughts crossing our minds.

When we turn out the lights
I see your homoerotic dreams
of a man across the ocean
and you detect my piercing
thoughts of a phantom spouse.
We both search and wonder:
Will we ever find a love
as comfortable as this?

Allegory of Fortune

—After the painting by Dosso Dossi

Fortune sits warily on a fragile bubble.
The winds of change, ready to transform
her direction, billow golden folds
of drapery around her. On her left foot,
only, a running shoe presses firmly
to the ground. She is poised, ready to flee.
Kneeling on her right knee, a bare
foot supports her delicate balance,
keeping her weight off the delicate orb;
one twist and Fortune's bubble might break.

She offers up to Chance a cornucopia
of abundance. Unfazed by her riches,
Chance smiles, clutching lottery tickets
in his right hand, ready to drop them
into the golden urn of fate. With his jewels
deftly hidden in red velvet, he faces
bare Fortune as her equal, both of them
desiring to bless the buyer, who bought
this seven-foot painting at a flea market
and strapped it to the roof of his car.

Transporting the metaphor, he sold
the canvas to Christie's Auction House
in New York City. Now displayed
at the Getty Museum in Los Angeles,
it sits in glory among the masters.
Far away from Ferrara, Italy,
far way from the 16th century,
the Allegory of Fortune
flaunts her perfect imagery,
with a charitable nod to Chance.

Kissing Mariyln Monroe's Crypt

I knew I belonged to the public and to the world, not because
I was talented or even beautiful, but because
I had never belonged to anything or anyone else.
                                    —Marilyn Monroe

In the Corridor of Memories, she
rests eternally, closed inside her crypt.

Bouquets of white roses and pure lilies
adorn the stone memorial façade now

covered in red and pink lipstick kisses,
neatly puckered and placed bright mementos

of devotion from her fans, visitors
and the occasional cross-dresser, who,

with tears cascading through his mascara,
is now kissing Marilyn Monroe's crypt.

Embarrassed, yet riveted, I witness
this intimate exhibit of female

adoration. Inhaling the faint scent
of Chanel Number 5, whirling around

us, he faces me and swirls his white dress,
adjusts his blonde wig and waves me forward.

Impulsively accepting his lavish
invitation, I take his manicured hand

and kiss her crypt, where I leave my coral
lip print and then Westwood Memorial Park,

playfully blowing my new friend a kiss,
while dreaming my long, brunette hair, blonde.

Awakened

You hold me in your arms until the pain
pills work their magic and the syncopated
rhythm of our breaths bends time.

There, in a war before we were born,
we helplessly clutch each other,
bombs falling around us, before we die.

Awakened by death, I open my eyes
and stare at the snow flurries strangely
illuminated by a full-faced moon.

The bouquet of white roses upon
the windowsill basks in pure radiance:
a midnight moment of enchantment.

Inhaling the sweetness of your breath
I glide back to sleep, content knowing
we are drifting through eternity.

IV.

And so desire carries me along.

"E cosi desio me mana."

—Petrarch

A Red Cherry on a White Tile Floor

—for Maram Al-Massri

Vibrant sexuality explodes
in your poems,
ripe and passionate
against your chaste
Syrian upbringing,
a stark dichotomy
like the title of your book,
the borrowed
title of this poem.

In a cult of veils you clung
to the idea of liberty, fleeing
eventually to Paris to bare
you arms, your thighs, and
your blood red heart
on the page.
Flirting with freedom
brought euphoria
mixed with sadness

as you unified
the sights and scents
of Arabic traditions,
dressed them in mini-
skirts and high heels
and strutted through
the literary world
a mix of racy rebellion
and subdued submission,

every woman emerging:
madonna and whore.

Nuda Veritas

In all things it is better to hope than to despair.
—Johann Wolfgang von Goethe

I open the white wooden shutters each
morning, listening to recorded chimes
from the Westwood Church. Radiant rays reach
my room warming my broken heart, lifetimes
of sadness now abandoned as I preach
to myself with unspoken lines of rhymes.
Awaiting the birth of grandson, Thomas,
I examine life: *nuda veritas.*

Here in Los Angeles, he will enter
this world among all the beautiful ones,
but there will be much more to his center.
Near UCLA, a young girl, someone's
daughter, sits with suitcases around her,
homeless, collecting food, clothing and tons
of books she reads in the warm open air
where people pass by her without a care.

Here, in this sun city, we wait with hope.
I walk to *Starbucks* each morning and sit
with Hai, who allows his old dog to cope
with the heat by lying in the cool wet
grass. We ponder the homeless horoscope
and marvel at the new sneakers on Brett,
the vagrant everyone knows by first name.
Thomas, you are the candle and the flame.

In this old world your light will shine anew.
Around us, white blossomed magnolia trees
drop pods of bright red berries, only few
surviving to reproduce new green leaves.
What to say of your half-brother I knew:
Oh, child of my own child, loss came in threes.
My first grandson murdered with his mother,
grief compounded by an unborn brother.

Like the apostle, Thomas, precariously
you'll balance zealous faith in tomorrow
with open-eyed doubt about what you see
in this world at war. Yet you must borrow
truth from where you find it unknowingly,
in the undertows of life and rainbow
arcs that hug the globe after rain. Thomas,
embrace life, this unpredictable promise.

The Illumination of Being

Do not fear the politicians
who spit out rhetoric,
as taut as the tight rope
upon which they balance
their positions.

Nor should you fear the actors,
who memorize the words of others
before contemplating
social injustice and finding
their true cause.

Neither fear the musician
whose music soothes or incites
for, with fame, he too may
seek out justice
for the poor and downtrodden.

Fear only the poets,
whose words sing mere songs,
For we, who have recorded
the rise and fall of Troy, observe
simple truths, pens poised in hope.

Our only desire:
the illumination of being.

Hero

Daddy didn't dare tell Mama
how to raise her three daughters,
specially, he didn't dare tell
her no Catholic Schools.

But, Daddy, brave man
who fought in the Philippines,
earned all his medals and my heart
when he waltzed into my third

grade classroom, lifted me into
his arms and danced past
shocked Sister Canisus.
Triumphant, Daddy didn't dare

go home. Instead, we went
to Joe's Bar and Grill, the local
gin mill, my Mama called it,
and I sipped pink soda

while Daddy downed courage.
Hours later, with audacity
and two ice cream cones,
we confronted the home front
where Mama screamed about

the school calling. Daddy didn't
dare scream back, only held my
hand tighter and kissed Mama's
reddening cheek then my nose.

Dianalee Velie

Falling asleep that night
in the translatable silence
that would torpedo our home
for months, I learned absence

of sound does not equal peace,
worlds exist beyond words,
and a hero's victory always involves
someone's ultimate defeat.

Flight

Do I
keep seeking out
the distant horizon,
blue, beckoning, and unclear or
do I

land here,
plunge into those
dark clouds below, faithful,
like a pilot on instruments
only,

that earth
will soon appear
beneath me, the solid,
unforgiving territory,
I know.

The Poet at Ten

Long brunette bangs, constantly pushed
behind her ears, hide her wandering green
eyes, eyes already bespectacled from
reading long after lights out and bedtime.

She's quiet in class, rarely raising her hand,
keeping her covert knowledge close to her
heart, never discussing the assignment or
answering seemingly unimportant questions.

She is too busy gazing out the window,
smiling at a ray of sunshine as it escorts
a passage of dust mites to the top of her
blank page, tickling her pen with delight.

So Many Shirts

She has stood and ironed so many shirts,
warm lumberjack plaids, proper business whites,
all sizes and shapes. Memories and hurts,
embedded in the fabric like parasites,

linger in the steam today, vaporized,
rising to mix with rare recollections
of the many men who monopolized
her goodwill, under certain conditions:

marriage, motherhood, lovers and live-ins.
Today she stands ironing and crying,
sprinkling our conversation with burdens
she holds tightly, hot resentments dying

to be burned out, allowing her pressing
needs to steam up into dreams of well-being.

Dianalee Velie

Burning the Past

Like a black butterfly boosted
by passionate ruby flames,

my charred personal identity
drifted into the evening sky,

floating with page after page
of her old address book,

pages having already succumbed
to the blaze in the roaring chiminea.

Red wine in our warming hands,
my friend continued to burn her past,

reciting a Litany of expletives:
dead, moved, lost all contact, also dead,

until she held my name in her hand,
and tossed the page on to the hearth,

where tongues of flames eagerly destroyed
my history to create the moment's warmth.

A truth, too simple to be spoken,
drifted into the evening air

with the delicate carbon filament, flitting
across the moon, disappearing among stars.

Clean Sweep

Romance swept past
us the day you gifted me
a vacuum cleaner
for my birthday.
I grant, you,
the old one
tired easily
and was lately
prone to violent outbursts
of dirt and dander,
the vacuum, that is,
not you, darling,
but the new one
came on bold and bright,
anxious to sweep up
anything in its path,
which is where
I placed myself
unknowingly anxious
to once again
be swept away.

Afloat in Paris

There are days when solitude is a heady wine that intoxicates you with freedom.
                                        —Colette

Afloat in Paris, I drift in my dream,
the Seine gently swaying l'Autobus,
the bells praying the twelve-noon angelus
from Notre Dame's towers rising upstream.

Rewriting the Book of Love, self-esteem
won at great expense, I am a nimbus
afloat in Paris. I drift in my dream,
the Seine gently swaying l'Autobus.

Single-mindedly catching a sunbeam,
surreal light surrounds my aloneness.
Content for the moment like Narcissus,
I am not as lonely as I may seem.
Afloat in Paris, I drift in my dream.

Twilight Ecstasy

Showcasing a carnival of cotton candy colors,
the early evening sky reflects sherbet swirls
across the lake where our boat, anchored
to the sand bar, floats in twilight ecstasy.

You, Thomas, ask dozens of questions,
which we, cocktail sipping adults, answer
with ease. *What's this? A compass. What's
this? A depth finder. What's this? A speaker.*

With melodies pin-wheeling in your eyes,
you chime, *turn on the music please,*
and we do. John Denver croons,
"you fill up my senses…" and then,

before he can sing, "a night in the forest,"
you take my sun-speckled hand
in your two-year-old smooth palm
and say, *Nonna, dance with me, please.*

Leading me to the bow of the boat,
you clasp my other hand and, following
your lead, we shift from foot to foot,
a private pas de deux rocking the boat

in the cradle of infinity. Under the big
top of the descending night sky,
the moon rises to spotlight our bond
and aerialist stars come out to spin

in this twilight ecstasy until the breeze
of the ringmasters benevolent breath
sweeps across the lake and this premiere
performance passes into eternity.

Adirondack Hours

We have left our everyday lives behind
to ponder Italian reflexive verbs,
imbibe in robust red wine, eat too much
and rock in the line up of rocking chairs
found on the front porch of the old farmhouse.

Listening to the still voice of nature
speak to us in Italian, all our needs
fulfilled by benevolent company,
in these Adirondack hours we rest,
immersed in the dailyness of being.

Ken, whose heart is bigger than the stent that
keeps it beating, lights the wood stove each dawn,
awakening us to a toasty hearth
and the aroma of fresh brewed coffee.
Coming down steep stairs that slant to the left,

we all wander to the kitchen table,
already bonded under Marie's roof,
in this house her father built, where she reigns
over us like the goddess mother earth
herself, hospitable and house warming.

Elizabetta, our own Minerva,
keeps us focused on expanding wisdom
with lesson plans and vocabulary
drills to heighten total comprehension
of this language we desire to share.

Sally, showering *al fresco*, barely
escapes being caught by a visiting
cousin, who thrills our evening with tales
of wild bears, runaway horses, plus
the story of two Italian brothers

who built this Adirondack get away,
where, on unexplored paths, Sally and I
create our own adventure, wandering
into an abandoned psychedelic
school bus covered in graffiti and leaves.

Back down the road a bit, the White Creek Boys
lay down their shotguns and ammunition
to whiff these aromatic smells drifting
in the woods: savory onions, garlic
and tomatoes, tempting to all, like apples
                                    in Paradise.

Love All

Poets have to love a game beginning
Love/All, Forty/Love, so close to winning,

the lack of a point signified by Love
under unconditional skies above.

Admiring your backhand return, I
stare at the ballistic ball transfixed by

its perfect placement in the left corner
bouncing hard and out of my reach, cleaner

than a slice of life. Such perfection in
motion, I do not run or try to win

this point. It is enough to watch the ball,
like a plunging sun, radiant downfall

of perfection and glory. Awaiting
another return, I bend low, fearing

I have misplaced my competitive edge
with an artist's eye and a poet's pledge

to love all beauty with intensity,
and honor ideal synchronicity,

to honor in verse, with this clear blue sky,
that holy shot, so it will never die.

Pink Moment

And so for the morning we practice being
eight years old again, two sisters pedaling
bicycles, yours powder blue with white daises,
mine innocent pink with creamy roses.

We fill our wicker baskets with adult treasures
of triple crème cheese, fresh mangoes and syrah
wine from the Ojai Valley, unlike the trinkets
from our past, Queen Anne's Lace, mica rocks
and the peanut butter and jelly sandwiches
we toted up Maple Avenue into the "woods,"
a patch of greenery in an industrial suburb,
where we played until the sun began to set
and Mom called us home for dinner.

Tonight we toast our bond with Pink Moment Martinis,
adult pink lemonade blended to reflect the rosy cast
of the Topa Topa Mountains at sunset,
soft, smooth mountains, that during the day seem
to roll in undulating waves of green-velvet sphagnum moss.
Remembering Mom, we vow to continue our spa reunions,
to be coddled, wrapped, massaged and rejuvenated,
until the day mom finally calls us home.

Dianalee Velie

Water Fire

—for Juliana and Will
            Providence, Rhode Island

Enraptured and respectful, like ancient Gods
before the River Styx, we pause in our stroll
along the blazing river to embrace
this dichotic scene: black wired baskets,
fueled with flaming logs, have set the river
afire, spreading a phosphorescent path in darkness.

We watch scarlet flames leap into the night
before tumbling into ebony waters
and disappearing. Volunteers, multiple
Charons dressed in ebony clothing,
deposit more logs on the radiant fires
from dark dinghies, blending with the charcoal

river and the matching sky. My friend rests
her head on her husband's shoulder and then,
they begin to dance, oblivious to the crowds
around them, as Jerome Kern's lyrics drift
lazily through the air with the gray smoke,
When a lovely flame dies/Smoke gets in you eyes.

They are bathed in the River Styx, exposed
and invulnerable. She has shed her
clerical collar, becoming, right now,
the River Goddess Styx, consumed with passion
for her parallel River God, Phlegethon,
both burning, yet not consumed by the others' fire.

Blinking back the sooty smoke in my eyes,
I allow this scene, this music and my own
River Lethe to wash away old memories,
lives and loves, as I hold your hand tighter,
bubbling with fires of desires,
crossing Hades into your warm arms.

The Alchemy of Desire

*The deepest level of truth, uncovered by science and by philosophy,
is the fundamental truth of unity. On that deepest subnuclear level of
our reality you and I are literally one.*
—John Hagelin, Quantum Physicist

From nothing and everything,
we split the cosmos with desire.
So shocked to be separated,
we reach across sun and moon,
searching for words to describe
this loss, words descending upon
our lips, silent, as celestial doves.
Bathed now in earthly weighted
waters, this new concrete world
surrounds us. Seeking the joy
of our original union, we cry out
with new pleasures, bringing us
very close, yet we remain divided.

And so we spend these years,
until tired of longing, we close
our eyes and rejoin the earth.
Closer now to unison, bodies
united in dust, our harmonies
converge, rising home
to the eternal realm.
As Gideon's dew anoints
our earthly mud, our spirit
descends into one perfected body
and we ascend, forever one,
knowing the power of love
reconstructs the universe,

allows it to:

appear and disappear
appear and disappear

eternally recreated,
dependent only,
upon the alchemy of desire.

Acknowledgments

Grateful acknowledgment to the publications in which these poems have
appeared or won awards

Aquila Review	"Clean Sweep"
Blueline	"Adirondack Hours"
Century 121	"A Red Cherry on a White Tile Floor"
Compass Rose	"Domestication"
Conceit Magazine	"Campus Highlights"
	"The Alchemy of Desire"
Conservative Blues	"Adirondack Hours"
	"Bar Harbor Fortune"
	"Holy Discord"
Deep Waters/Outrider Press	"Afloat in Paris"
Entelechy International	"Epiphany"
	"At Odds"
Fearsome Fascinations	"He Says"
Flesh & Spirit	"The Ecstasy of St.Thersa"
Heartbeat	"Of Sparrows and Men"
Ice Cream Stand Anthology	"Bad Date.com"
	"Body Parts"
	"Burning the Past"
	"Domestication"
	"Exalting the X Chromosome"
Inkwell	"Fog"
	"Spirit of Lake George"
	"Nuda Veritas"
Inspirit	"Blue Mountain Ecstasy"
	"Cold Desire"
Journey to Crone	"Pink Moment"
Ledge Magazine	"Spinach"
Manorborn	"Desiring Heaven"
	"Mirage in May"
Naugatuck River Review	"Kissing Marilyn Monroe's Crypt"
New Millennium Writings	"Love All"
Off the Coast	"Abenaki Morning Prayer"
Pen Woman	"Burning the Past"
Poet's Guide to New Hampshire, 2010	"Chicken Farmer I still Love You"
Poet's Touchstone	"Hero"
Sensations Magazine	"Abenaki Morning Prayer"
	"Bad Date.Com"
	"Pink Moment"
	"Portrait of the Poet"
	"Twilight Ecstasy"
Umbrellashoot	"Mrs. Wakefield"
Visions with Love	"Dandelions"
Where Beach Meets Ocean	"Morning Sacrament"
Without Halos	"In My Garden"

About the Author

Photo by Robert Jenks, Jenks Studio of Photography, 1204 Main St, St. Johsbery VT 05819

Dianalee Velie lives and writes in Newbury, New Hampshire. She is a graduate of Sarah Lawrence College, and has a Master of Arts in Writing from Manhattanville College, where she has served as faculty advisor of *Inkwell: A Literary Magazine*. She has taught poetry, memoir, and short story at universities and colleges in New York, Connecticut and New Hampshire and in private workshops throughout the United States, Canada and Europe. Her award-winning poetry and short stories have been published in hundreds of literary journals and many have been translated into Italian. She enjoys traveling to rural school systems in Vermont and New Hampshire teaching poetry for the Children's Literacy Foundation.

Velie's play, *Mama Says*, was directed by Daniel Quinn in a staged reading in New York City. She is the author of three prior books of poetry, *Glass House, First Edition*, and *The Many Roads to Paradise* published by Rock Village Publishing in Middleborough, Massachusetts. In 2010 Velie authored *Soul Proprietorship: Women in Search of Their Souls*, a collection of short stories published by Plain View Press in Austin Texas. *The Alchemy of Desire*, is her fourth poetry collection and is also also published by Plain View Press. She is a long time member of the National League of American Pen Women.

CPSIA information can be obtained
at www.ICGtesting.com
Printed in the USA
LVOW04s1519040416

482086LV00005B/124/P